This coloring book belongs to

○○○○○○○○○○○○○○○○○○○○○○○○○○○○○○○○○○○○○

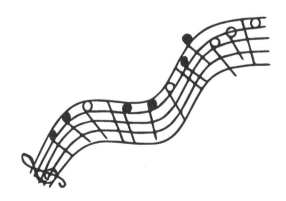

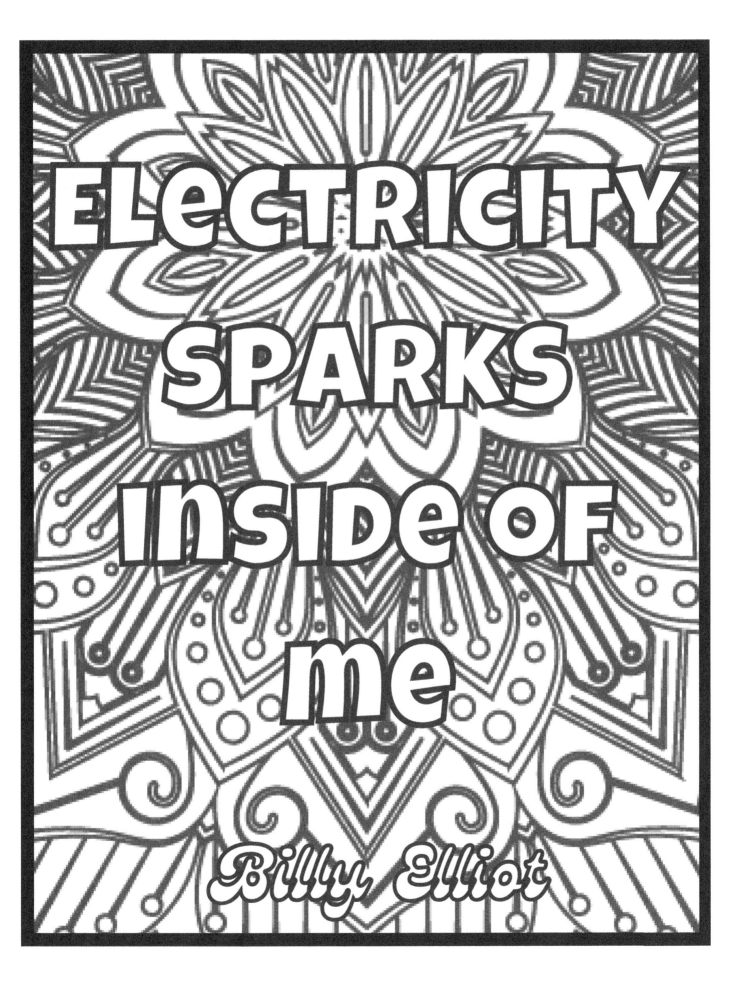

DON'T DREAM IT, BE IT

The Rocky Horror Picture Show

Don't it go
to show
ya never
know?

Little Shop of Horrors

Courage cannot erase our fear Courage is when we face our fear

Newsies

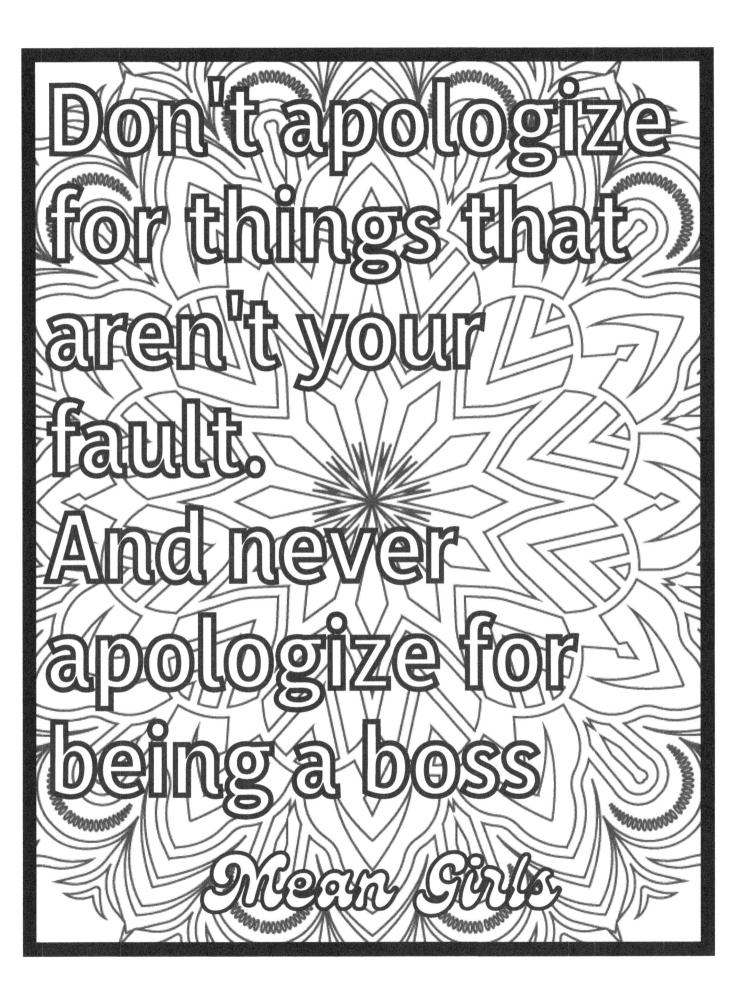

This book will
change your life

This book will
change your life

This book will
change your life

This book will
change your life

This book will
change your life

the Book of Mormon

YOU DECIDE WHAT'S RIGHT

YOU DECIDE WHAT'S GOOD

Into the Woods

GIVE 'EM THE OLD Razzle Dazzle

Chicago

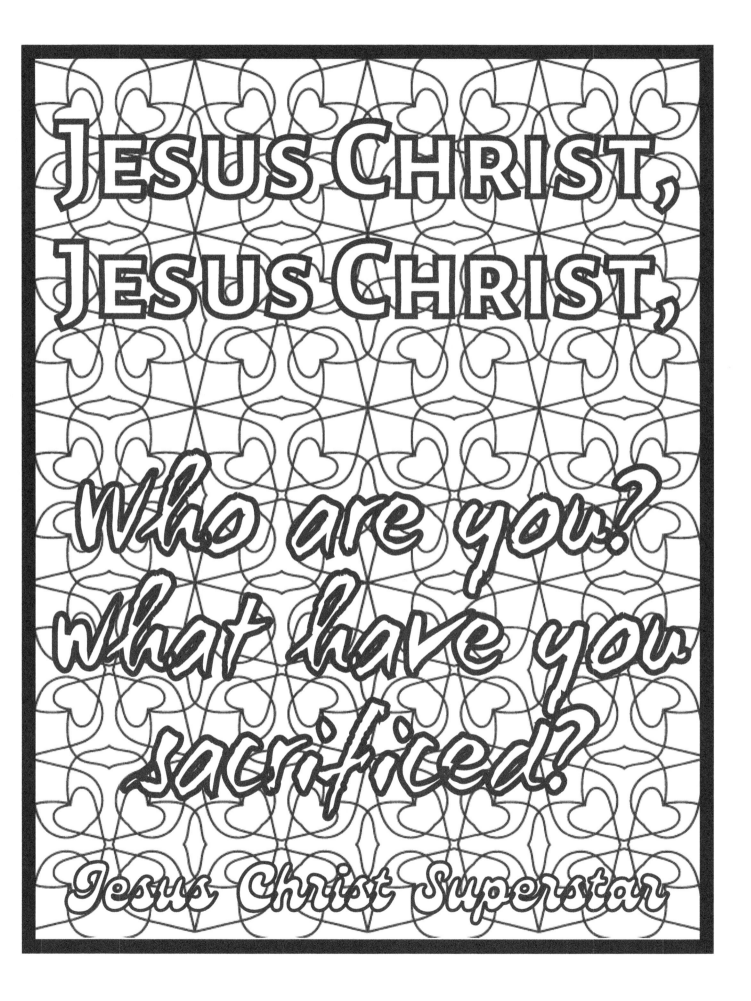

YOU WILL BE FOUND

Dear Evan Hansen

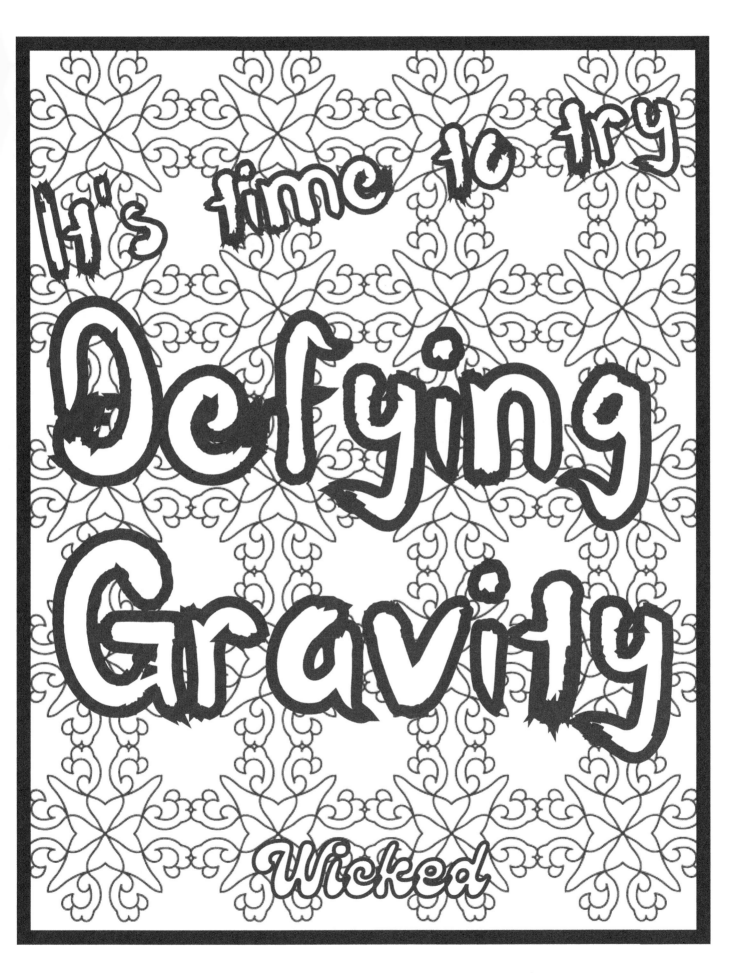

Made in United States
North Haven, CT
08 September 2023

41328702R00024